BIOINDICATOR SPECIES

FROGS
MATTER

by Tammy Gagne

Content Consultant
Elizabeth Davidson, PhD
School of Life Sciences
Arizona State University

Core Library

An Imprint of Abdo Publishing
abdopublishing.com

abdopublishing.com

Published by Abdo Publishing, a division of ABDO, PO Box 398166, Minneapolis, Minnesota 55439. Copyright © 2016 by Abdo Consulting Group, Inc. International copyrights reserved in all countries. No part of this book may be reproduced in any form without written permission from the publisher. Core Library™ is a trademark and logo of Abdo Publishing.

Printed in the United States of America, North Mankato, Minnesota
072015
012016

Cover Photo: iStockphoto
Interior Photos: iStockphoto, 1, 16 (top left), 16 (top right), 16 (center), 16 (bottom right), 16 (bottom left), 28; Brandon Alms/Shutterstock Images, 4; Red Line Editorial, 6; Andrew Lundquist/Shutterstock Images, 8; Frans Lanting/Corbis, 10; Doug Lemke/iStockphoto, 12, 43; Kat Paws/iStockphoto, 14; Stoyko Sabotanov/iStockphoto, 18; Matej Ziak/Shutterstock Images, 20; Shutterstock Images, 24; M. Rolands/iStockphoto, 26, 45; Eugene Hoshiko/AP Images, 30; Lewis Jackson/iStockphoto, 32; Kenneth Graff/Shutterstock Images, 34; Peter Komka/EPA/Newscom, 36; Peter Bennett/Citizen of the Planet/Newscom, 38

Editor: Jon Westmark
Series Designer: Laura Polzin

Library of Congress Control Number: 2015945398

Cataloging-in-Publication Data
Gagne, Tammy.
 Frogs matter / Tammy Gagne.
  p. cm. -- (Bioindicator species)
ISBN 978-1-68078-011-6 (lib. bdg.)
Includes bibliographical references and index.
1. Frogs--Juvenile literature. 2. Frog ecology--Juvenile literature.   3. Environmental protection--Juvenile literature.   I. Title.
597.8--dc23

                                                                    2015945398

CONTENTS

CHAPTER ONE

AN IMPORTANT MESSAGE

After a long day of catching flies, the frogs have settled in for their nightly routine. Even before the sun has set in the western United States, the croaking begins. *Ribbit! Ribbit!* Although many people think all frogs make this sound, only male Pacific tree frogs actually do. Other frogs croak in different ways—and for a variety of reasons. Many times they are singing to attract females. Other times their

For many frog species, such as the red-eyed tree frog, only the males call.

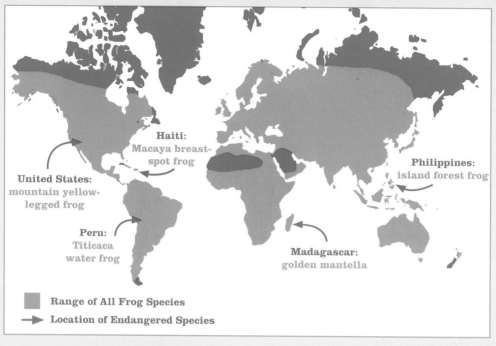

United States:
mountain yellow-
legged frog

Haiti:
Macaya breast-
spot frog

Philippines:
island forest frog

Peru:
Titicaca
water frog

Madagascar:
golden mantella

Range of All Frog Species
Location of Endangered Species

Around the World

Just as frogs live throughout the world, various frog species around the globe are at risk of dying out. How does seeing the map help you understand the problems facing frogs?

croaking means they are claiming land as their own. Frogs may even croak to express fear or announce that a storm is on its way. With this one sound, frogs can say quite a bit.

Frogs also say things in another important way. Frogs are bioindicators. Scientists study these animals to measure the health of the environment. Healthy frogs are a sign that the surrounding wildlife is also thriving.

Where the Frogs Are

Frogs live on nearly every continent around the world. Antarctica is the only continent in which they are not found. The climate there is too cold and dry. But approximately 4,740 frog species live on the other six continents. Frog populations are highest in tropical regions. The tropics are the warm areas just north and south of the equator.

Just as frogs prefer warmth, most frogs also do best near water. Frogs are amphibians. This means they live in water and breathe through gills for the first part of their lives. For this reason, ponds are ideal spots for most frog species. Plants that grow near ponds help frogs in several ways. They give frogs shelter from harsh weather and from predators, such as snakes and birds. Plants also keep areas moist by giving them shade. Frogs move to land and breathe

Frogs prefer moist, shaded areas to stay cool and take in water.

with lungs as adults. But they still need moisture to survive.

A frog's skin takes in moisture. Most animals cannot survive without drinking water. A frog gets all the water it needs just by spending time in the water. But these animals also absorb substances in the water. Sometimes water has chemicals in it. A frog's skin also soaks these up.

What Is Happening to Frogs?

Healthy frogs are a good sign. But sick frogs are a warning that an ecosystem is in danger. For example, frogs often develop sicknesses, such as cancer, when chemicals such as pesticides enter the water. Some frogs even grow extra or deformed limbs. Frogs' failing health tells researchers that a waterway is becoming polluted. As frogs become ill or die, other species usually follow. If people swim in or drink the water, they too can become sick.

Frogs even serve as bioindicators when they are not nearby. In many

Two for One

As amphibians, frogs live part of their lives in water and part on land. The word *amphibian* comes from the Greek word *amphibia*, which means "living a double life." Most frogs begin as tadpoles. These tiny creatures breathe through gills as fish do. Tadpoles lose their tails and develop lungs for breathing air as they grow into adult frogs. Because of this change, frogs live in two different environments during their lifetimes. Scientists who study frogs learn much about two different ecosystems in the process.

Frog deformities often indicate environmental problems.

areas where certain frog species were once plentiful, they are becoming scarce. Some species are slowly dying out. Their disappearance tells humans that something is wrong. Often the issue is pollution. Other times the problem is that people have moved into the animals' habitat, forcing the frogs to move.

Since 1980, 120 amphibian species have disappeared from Earth. These include species of frogs, toads, and salamanders. More species could also become extinct if people do not work to save them. Experts predict that seven frog species in the United

PERSPECTIVES
Biology 101

Dissecting frogs has been part of biology courses for many years. Many of these frogs are farm raised. But a significant number are taken from the wild. In 2012 more than 300,000 frogs were caught in Mexico to be used for dissection. Computers have made it possible for students to do virtual dissections. But many schools are not using the computer method. Some teachers insist it is not as good. They argue it does not give students the same experience as the real thing.

The Panamanian golden frog of the Central American rain forests is just one of many endangered frog species.

States will lose half their populations in just seven years if nothing changes. Their ecosystems will also suffer from these losses.

Frogs play an important role in keeping the world clean and free of disease. For example, tadpoles feed on algae, making water cleaner. Adult frogs eat mosquitoes, which can carry diseases. By allowing frog populations to decline, people could be placing their own health at risk. Everything in the ecosystem is connected. Paying attention to the signs these valuable species are sending can help humans save much more than just one type of animal.

EXPLORE ONLINE

Go to the website below and read about why studying frogs is important. How does this information compare with what you have read in Chapter One? Write a paragraph describing what we can learn about the environment from observing frogs. Use facts to back up your opinion.

FrogWatch
mycorelibrary.com/frogs-matter

CHAPTER TWO

WHY ARE FROGS IN TROUBLE?

Amphibians are among the most endangered animals on Earth. Nearly one-third of these animals are at risk of dying out. Frogs are declining in number for several reasons. Some species are losing their homes. Others are being harmed by pollution. Rising temperatures around the world are also hurting these animals. Many species are affected by more than one of these problems.

Frogs breathe through their skin, making water pollution a major threat.

The Wetlands Ecosystem
Frogs are just one of many life-forms that are part of the wetland ecosystem. This diagram shows some possible predator-prey relationships. The arrows show the flow of energy through the ecosystem. Based on the diagram, how might the decline of frogs affect other animals in the ecosystem?

Habitat Loss

One of the biggest threats to frogs is the loss of their

habitats. More than 7 billion people live on Earth.

As the human population has gone up, people have begun using more and more of Earth's resources. This process often hurts the plants and animals in the area. Houses and other buildings are built. And the surrounding wetlands are often destroyed. When this happens, frogs and other wildlife are forced to leave the area.

Unlike animals with wings, frogs must search for new homes on foot. If there is no clean water nearby, their future quickly becomes grim. Many frogs do not survive the journey to find a new habitat. Some frogs do reach new locations. But there they have to compete for food and space with other frog species.

Wind and rain can bring pesticides to wet areas where frogs live.

Even where water levels are slightly lowered, frogs can still suffer. Like frogs, many insects live in or near water. Less water means fewer insects for frogs and tadpoles to eat. A smaller habitat also means more frogs compete for limited food.

When people and businesses move into wetlands, they usually remove fallen trees, piles of leaves, and small plants in the area. People might see these items as unimportant or even useless. But frogs and other animals rely on them for shelter.

In the Air and the Water

Pollution is harmful to many species, including humans. But frogs are among the first species to suffer from dangerous chemicals that enter Earth's waterways. When farmers or gardeners use pesticides, these substances reach more than just the plants. Rainwater washes pesticides to the ground. The chemicals then travel downhill with the rainwater until they reach a body of water. Once pollution makes it into a waterway, it can travel even faster and farther.

Tadpoles exposed to chemicals could develop disorders before becoming adults.

Many pesticides are sprayed onto plants. This allows wind to carry them beyond their original location. When this happens, the chemicals can travel great distances even if it does not rain for days or weeks. Evaporation can also transport the pollutants. The sun's warmth can turn the chemicals into gases, which float up to the clouds. The chemicals then fall back to Earth with the rain.

After absorbing pesticides through their skin, frogs may react in a variety of ways. Pesticides can keep tadpoles from developing into adult frogs. In the worst cases, frogs die from exposure to chemicals. Pollutants also hurt frogs' immune systems. A poor immune system puts the frogs at a greater risk for diseases, such as ranaviruses. This group of illnesses strikes cold-blooded animals, killing large numbers of them. Humans have made the spread of these diseases worse by using frogs as fishing bait. When a diseased frog enters the water, other amphibians can catch the disease.

Climate Change

As people take over more land, Earth loses many plants. Plants help clean the air by taking up gases,

Making Them Sick

The Sierra Nevada yellow-legged frog is the most endangered frog in the United States. Many members of this species are suffering from an infection called chytrid fungus. The disease has already caused 100 other amphibian species around the world to go extinct. Some scientists think warming temperatures have increased the spread of the illness.

such as carbon dioxide. Automobiles, power plants, and factories produce this harmful gas. Too much carbon dioxide in the air raises temperatures over time. This problem is called climate change. And with fewer plants to take in gases like carbon dioxide, the temperature continues to go up.

As temperatures rise, wetlands are drying up. This change takes habitat away from frogs and other animals. In tropical regions, for example, some frogs lay their eggs in moist leaf piles instead of water. These species skip the tadpole stage. They hatch as tiny frogs, called froglets. But if the soil is too dry, the froglets cannot survive.

As people destroy wetlands, they also lose important natural resources. People need clean water for drinking, bathing, and washing clothes and dishes. Pollution in the water can also make people sick. On a larger scale, climate change threatens living things around the planet. The very things that are hurting frogs are also hurting the rest of the world.

FURTHER EVIDENCE

There is quite a bit of information about what is happening to frogs in Chapter Two. What was one of the chapter's main points? What evidence was given to support that point? Check out the website at the link below. Choose a quote from the website that relates to this chapter. Does this quote support the chapter's main point? Does it make a new point? Write a few sentences explaining how the quote you found relates to this chapter.

PBS Nature: The World's Most Endangered Frogs
mycorelibrary.com/frogs-matter

CHAPTER THREE

WHY FROGS MATTER

As bioindicators, frogs give incredible information about the environment. Even people who are not big fans of amphibians should be pleased when they see or hear frogs nearby. It means that the air, soil, and water are healthy for life in general. When frogs are suffering, it is often a sign that other species are also in danger. These amphibians offer insight into the health of their ecosystems.

Frogs' close relationship with water tells humans a lot about the environment.

If too much algae grows in ponds, tadpoles may not be able to get enough oxygen from the water to survive.

Don't Drink the Water

People must pay close attention when frogs are displaced due to pollution. Drinking from polluted water sources is risky for both people and animals. But it is not just the water that could be dangerous.

Sometimes tadpoles and frogs in the water seem healthy, but frogs on land are suffering. In these cases, the air or soil could be polluted. And if one ecosystem is polluted, those nearby are likely to follow. For example, many frogs disappear from the banks of a pond because of pollution. This means they can no longer lay eggs in nearby water. Tadpoles play a big role in keeping water clean by eating algae. Without tadpoles, algae grow more abundantly. But these plants also die quickly. As the dead algae decompose, they remove oxygen from the water. Fish and other aquatic animals cannot survive if oxygen levels fall too low. Algae can also add toxins to water. This can make the water unsafe for drinking or swimming.

The disappearance of adult frogs can cause insect populations to go up. Like frogs, mosquitoes

PERSPECTIVES
A Vital Resource

Frogs have become an important part of medical research. These amphibians produce a number of fluids through their skins. Researchers have found that some of these substances can be used to make medicines. About 10 percent of Nobel Prizes in physiology and medicine have come from research about frogs. If just one frog species living today goes extinct, the world could lose an important cure that has not yet been discovered.

Frogs eat flies and mosquitoes, which helps stop the spread of disease.

breed in water. Frogs living near water help keep mosquito populations under control. Without frogs, mosquitoes and other insect populations may quickly rise. Certain other animals eat insects. Dragonflies, for example, eat large numbers of mosquitoes and other bugs. But if frogs are suffering, other living things—such as dragonflies—are likely in trouble as well. These larger insects depend on water as much as frogs do. As water pollution hurts frogs, it also endangers dragonflies.

A Warming Trend

As Earth continues to warm, many animals and plants are declining in number. The things frogs tell us about climate change affect all living things. This includes other animal species and humans. We share the planet with frogs and other wildlife, so what hurts their habitat also hurts ours.

When scientists note a decrease in frogs due to climate change, it is no small matter. Frogs are among the first species affected by climate change, but they

A shell lies in a dried-up wetland during a severe drought in China.

are far from the last. As the air warms, smaller bodies of water dry up. This can be like a death sentence for wildlife that depends on these water sources.

By studying frogs, researchers are learning how climate change is affecting both animals and the environment. Four amphibious species live in

Yellowstone National Park in the western United States. Three of these species' populations are down, including the Columbia spotted frog. Scientists blame the increasing number of droughts for this drop in population. One-quarter of the ponds in Yellowstone no longer fill with rainwater. This is making it harder for frogs and other amphibians to survive. The danger these animals are facing is a striking example of how climate change is affecting wildlife.

Helping Humans

Even people who do not come across frogs benefit from them. Frogs eat mosquitoes and other insects. This means they play an important role in keeping the human population healthy. Mosquitoes can spread diseases, particularly malaria. Without frogs these insects would increase in numbers. As a result, people would face a higher risk of serious illness.

Droughts in the western United States are also affecting people. One does not need to live nearby to suffer from the results. Lack of rain makes it more

Droughts can have a major impact on farmers and the economy.

difficult for farmers to grow crops. Growers often lose large amounts of fruits and vegetables after droughts. This loss means less money for the farmers. It also means less food for buyers and higher prices at the supermarket.

Scientists who study frogs have been noticing a sharp drop in populations. They have also noticed a rise in deformities in certain frog species. Writer and professor John Marshall explains why these problems are cause for concern, even for the average person:

> *What does all this have to do with the health of your garden? Whatever affects amphibians also may affect people. Because frogs, toads and salamanders are so sensitive to pollutants, and because they are so much smaller than humans, they will likely show signs of problems in your garden before it affects you. They can serve the same function that canaries used to serve for coal miners years ago: Being more sensitive to poisonous gases than the humans, when the canary became sick or died, the miners knew something was wrong.*
>
> Source: John Marshall. "Indicator Species: Using Frogs and Salamanders to Gauge Ecosystem Health." Grit. Ogden Publications, August 2013. Web. Accessed June 1, 2015.

What's the Big Idea?

Take a close look at this text. What is the main point? Pick out two details used to make this point. What can you tell about frogs and pollution based on this text?

CHAPTER FOUR

MOVING FORWARD

Some people learn about frogs because they find them interesting or cool. They want to find a way to save the animals. Others care more about the environment and want to keep climate change from altering the planet. Working toward either of these goals helps the other one. By saving frogs, we may also help the environment.

Learning about frogs is a great way to learn about other parts of the environment too.

Volunteers in Hungary look for frogs along a barrier designed to keep frogs from crossing a busy highway.

In the Works

Many organizations work to save Earth's endangered animals. But fewer specialize in saving frogs. Save the Frogs is the world's only nonprofit focused on saving amphibians. This organization has created a breeding program. Members hope it will help save threatened or endangered frog species.

Other organizations also work to save amphibians. Amphibian Ark is made up of several different groups, including the World Association of Zoos and Aquariums. Like Save the Frogs, this joint project works to save threatened amphibian species.

Larger organizations, such as Greenpeace, also play an important role in helping frogs. These groups educate people about environmental problems, such as climate change. From the Arctic to the rain forests, Greenpeace also works to save natural resources and slow climate change. One

PERSPECTIVES
Different Opinions

Not all researchers agree when it comes to climate change. Some scientists argue that temperatures rise and fall naturally over long periods of time. They also think people are reading too much into the connection between bioindicator species and climate change. Many other scientists insist the evidence of climate change speaks for itself. For example, tropical air temperatures between 1975 and 2000 rose three times faster than the average for the century.

Preventing litter is one way people can help frogs.

way it does this is through the PolluterWatch Project. The project draws attention to businesses that are adding to the climate change problem. This attention puts pressure on companies to make the environment a bigger priority.

What Else Is Needed?

Donating time or money to a conservation group is a great way to help both frogs and the environment. But people do not have to join an organization to make a difference. They can start by making small changes in their routines.

Recycling, for example, keeps trash from building up in rivers and other waterways. Many people choose to make a difference by buying items that can be used again instead of being thrown away. Cutting chemical use also helps reduce pollution. Toxic products, such as air fresheners and cleaners, hurt the earth. Environmentally friendly products have a lesser impact.

One of the best ways to help frogs is by saving water. People who leave the water running while brushing their teeth can help by simply turning the faucet off. Likewise, they can limit their shower time to just a few minutes each day. Collecting rainwater for gardening instead of using a hose also saves water. As people learn about the ways they can help the environment, they can share what they know with family and friends. Each person can make a difference.

The Future of Frogs

No one knows for sure what the future holds for many frog species. Much depends on the efforts humans make to reduce climate change. People must also take the information these bioindicators are revealing seriously. The good news is that frogs can help measure progress in slowing climate change. When frogs that are endangered start increasing in number, the environment is moving in the right direction.

One thing that is difficult to deny is that frogs are among the first animals affected when the climate changes. If people do not want to lose certain species to extinction, they must take action to save them.

Only time will tell the extent to which humans are affecting the climate. In the meantime, people will keep studying bioindicator species, the environment, and the links between them.

Not Gone Yet

In 1996 the Hula painted frog became the first amphibian to be listed as extinct. But a 2011 patrol through Israel's wetlands had a surprising discovery: The species was not completely gone. A male frog of the species was found in the valley. While this species is far from out of danger, ten more members of the species have turned up in the same area.

Fifteen-year-old Eve Nilson traveled to Brazil to study frogs and other rain forest animals. In an interview, she described her thoughts on saving the rain forest, an important frog habitat:

Kids can do a lot in their hometown. You can start or join an environmental club. You can always write to government representatives and encourage them to help. You have an opinion and it's important to voice your opinion. Donate to foundations that help rain forests. Also talk to your friends about how important the rain forest is to you as a person. By talking about how important the rain forest is, you can promote awareness. There are also alternatives to products that are produced from the rain forest and endangered species. It's important to buy products that are environmentally safe.

Source: Eve Nilson. "Live Online Interview with Eve Nilson." Scholastic. Scholastic Inc., April 2015. Web. Accessed June 1, 2015.

Consider Your Audience

Imagine that you are trying to convince your parents that they too can help the environment. How might you use the information in this passage for this purpose? What kinds of things do you think you could do together to help save frogs and their ecosystems?

Common Name: Frog

Scientific Name: Anura

Average Size: 1 to 8 inches (2.5–20 cm) long

Average Weight: 7 ounces (198 g)

Color: Many colors and patterns

Average Life Span: Up to 15 years

Diet: Insects, such as flies, mosquitoes, and moths; algae

Habitat: Wetlands

Predators: Fish, crayfish, birds, otters, snakes

What's Happening: Many frog populations are decreasing.

Where It's Happening: Every continent except Antarctica

Why It's Happening: Land development, pollution, disease, and climate change are hurting frogs and their habitats.

Why It's Important: The decreasing frog population is a sign that the environment is in trouble.

What You Can Do:

- Write a letter to your state representative. Explain the importance of frogs as bioindicators.
- Conserve energy and water each day and encourage others to do so as well.
- Donate money to or volunteer with an environmental organization that works to protect frogs and other bioindicator species.

STOP AND THINK

Surprise Me

Chapter One shared a lot of information about frogs as a bioindicator species. List two or three facts from the chapter you found most surprising. Why did they surprise you?

Take a Stand

What do you think is the best way to spread the word about what is happening to frogs and the environment? Write a letter to someone you think can help make a difference. Urge that person to get involved. Perhaps the person is a local or national politician. Even a celebrity such as an actor, singer, or athlete might be able to adopt these causes and help educate others about bioindicators.

Tell the Tale

Write 200 words from the point of view of a frog that was forced to leave its habitat due to pollution. Make sure to set the scene, develop a sequence of events, and include a conclusion.

You Are There

Imagine you are a biologist doing research in wetlands. What might you notice about the water you see? What signs might signal that the frogs are in trouble? What does this information tell you about the surrounding environment?

GLOSSARY

algae
plantlike organisms that grow in water

conservation
the preservation and protection of a plant, animal, or habitat

dissect
to cut into separate parts for examination and study

ecosystem
a community of living things interacting with their environment

evaporation
the process of liquid changing into vapor

immune system
the body's natural defense against foreign substances, cells, and tissues

nonprofit
an organization that does not make money after expenses have been paid

pesticide
a substance used to kill pests

ranavirus
a group of diseases that affect cold-blooded animals

tadpole
the larva of a frog, which breathes with gills and lives in water

LEARN MORE

Books

Moore, Robin. *In Search of Lost Frogs: The Quest to Find the World's Rarest Amphibians*. Richmond Hill, Ontario: Firefly Books, 2014.

Simon, Seymour. *Frogs*. New York: HarperCollins, 2015.

Turner, Pamela S. *The Frog Scientist*. Boston: HMH Books for Young Readers, 2011.

Websites

To learn more about Bioindicator Species, visit **abdopublishing.com**. These links are routinely monitored and updated to provide the most current information available.

Visit **mycorelibrary.com** for free additional tools for teachers and students.

INDEX

ABOUT THE AUTHOR

Tammy Gagne is the author of more than 100 books for adults and children. She resides in northern New England with her husband and son. One of her favorite pastimes is visiting schools to speak to kids about writing.